D1251782

# GREAT MINDS
## of Ancient Science and Math

# MEASURING THE EARTH

## ERATOSTHENES AND HIS CELESTIAL GEOMETRY

Mary Gow

**Enslow Publishers, Inc.**
40 Industrial Road
Box 398
Berkeley Heights, NJ 07922
USA
http://www.enslow.com

**Library of Congress Cataloging-in-Publication Data**

Gow, Mary.
    Measuring the Earth : Eratosthenes and his celestial geometry / Mary Gow.
        p. cm. — (Great minds of ancient science and math)
    Includes bibliographical references and index.
    Summary: "A biography of ancient Greek mathematician Eratosthenes, who used geometry
to calculate the circumference of the earth. He is also known as the Father of Geography"—
Provided by publisher.
    ISBN-13: 978-0-7660-3120-3
    ISBN-10: 0-7660-3120-9
    1. Eratosthenes—Juvenile literature. 2. Mathematicians—Greece—Biography—Juvenile
literature. 3. Astronomers—Greece—Biography—Juvenile literature 4. Earth—Figure—
Measurement—Juvenile literature 5. Arc measures—Juvenile literature. 6. Mathematics,
Ancient—Juvenile literature 7. Mathematics, Greek—Juvenile literature. I. Title.
    QA31.E7G69 2010
    510.92—dc22
    [B]
                                        2008038523

Printed in the United States of America

10 9 8 7 6 5 4 3 2 1

**To Our Readers:** We have done our best to make sure all Internet addresses in this book were active
and appropriate when we went to press. However, the author and the publisher have no control over
and assume no liability for the material available on those Internet sites or on other Web sites they may
link to. Any comments or suggestions can be sent by e-mail to comments@enslow.com or to the
address on the back cover.

♻ Enslow Publishers, Inc., is committed to printing our books on recycled paper. The paper in every
book contains 10% to 30% post-consumer waste (PCW). The cover board on the outside of each book
contains 100% PCW. Our goal is to do our part to help young people and the environment too!

**Illustration Credits:** Wikimedia Commons, pp. 8, 18, 20, 28, 33, 40, 68 ; Principal Coins
of the Ancients, p. 23 ; Collection of Samuel Jean de Pozzi, p. 33, Lizzy Hewitt, pp. 25, 96;
Images courtesy History of Science Collections, University of Oklahoma Libraries;
copyright the Board of Regents of the University of Oklahoma, pp. 49, 50, 99, 100 ; Anna
Hagen, p. 51; Jeannie Sargent, pp. 54, 81, 84, 86; Geography of Strabo, p. 73.

**Cover Illustration:** The Image Works

# CONTENTS

# "PENTATHLOS"

THE SAILOR FROM GENOA EXPECTED HIS voyage to change the world. Opening a new route to Asia would bring much desired spices like cinnamon and pepper to Europe. The adventurer had no silly worries about falling off the edge of the world. Europeans knew that the earth was round. The sailor's concern was the length of the voyage. To anticipate the distance his ships and sailors would need to travel, he sought out books with information about the world's geography.

*Historia Rerum Ubique Gestarum* was one of the books that Christopher Columbus studied. A collection of world knowledge at the time, its Latin title translates to "history of things everywhere." Columbus had his own copy of this encyclopedia-like volume that was published in 1477. Carefully reading its pages, he wrote detailed notes in its margins.[1] In *Historia Rerum*, Columbus read Eratosthenes' measurement of the earth's circumference. Eratosthenes, a brilliant ancient Greek, had calculated the size of Earth about seventeen hundred years before Columbus was planning out his journey. Eratosthenes used observations and mathematics for his measurement.

Christopher Columbus chose to believe sources other than Eratosthenes. He accepted a calculation that made the earth about 25 percent smaller than Eratosthenes claimed. He also believed that the landmass of Europe and Asia was larger than ancient sources suggested. With Columbus's adjustments of a smaller earth and bigger land, the distance across the seas did not seem so great.[2] Had Columbus believed the ancient Greek, when his ships bumped into land in October 1492, he would have known that he was in a "New World," not in Asia.

In the third century B.C., Eratosthenes determined that the earth's circumference was 252,000 stades. Stades were an ancient unit of measurement. Scholars still haggle about whether Eratosthenes used an Olympic stade, an Egyptian stade, or a stade of some other length. Using Egyptian measurements, (he was in Egypt at the time), his 252,000 stades equal 24,663 miles (39,691 kilometers). This compares to the modern calculation of the earth's circumference at the equator as 24,902 miles (40,075 kilometers).[3] Even if Eratosthenes was not that stunningly accurate, using other measurements for the stade, his calculation was still within about three thousand miles (forty-eight hundred kilometers).

Measuring the earth so precisely was an impressive feat. However, it was only one of Eratosthenes' many remarkable achievements.

Eratosthenes was born in Cyrene, a prosperous Greek city on the Mediterranean coast of North Africa. As a young man, he went to Athens to study. His enduring fame comes

ERATOSTHENES
Ex Dactylioth Lippert.

No statues or other images of Eratosthenes exist from his lifetime. Nor are there any descriptions of his appearance. This is an artist's impression of what the geographer and librarian may have looked like.

from his many productive years in Alexandria, Egypt, the intellectual and cultural center of the world at the time. There, he was a member of the royal court of the Greek kings who ruled Egypt. He served the kings of the Ptolemy family as director of the great Library of Alexandria. At the library, Eratosthenes had the collected knowledge of the known world at his fingertips.

Eratosthenes' achievements were far ranging. He is most famous for his studies of the earth and is often called the "Father of Geography." Using mathematics to study the earth, he broke new ground. In his monumental three-volume *Geographica*, he took a global view of the world. With its title, he coined a new word—geography. In this book, he described the inhabited earth, its lands and people. Setting aside mythological and traditional views of lands, he used written descriptions of military campaigns and observations by travelers to try to find distances between places. Looking beyond the earth, he measured the angle through which the sun shifts from south to north between midwinter and

9

midsummer. This measurement corresponds to what we now know as the tilt of the earth's axis relative to the plane of its orbit around the sun.

A mathematician of note, Eratosthenes wrote at least two books on the subject, titled *On Means* and *Platonicus*.[4] He devised a tool, now called the Sieve of Eratosthenes, for finding prime numbers. Of all his mathematical work, he was especially proud of his solution to a famous math problem. Known as the "Delian problem," it required finding a way to exactly double the volume of a cube. Eratosthenes commissioned a public monument that he dedicated to the king with his solution to this problem.

Eratosthenes' creativity was not limited to math and geography. He established a chronology, a system of dating events in ancient Greece. His system, adapted by later Greeks and Romans, forms the framework of our knowledge of many dates from that era. A theater fan, he wrote a well-respected twelve-book series, *Ancient Comedy*. Like many educated Greeks of the time, he wrote poetry. One of his poems offered a look at Earth as seen from the heavens. Eratosthenes' *Catasterisms* recorded the myths behind the Greeks' constellations and described their layout in the sky.

Eratosthenes' story is closely tied to the story of the library he led. The Library at Alexandria was one of the true treasures of the ancient world. The first of its kind, it was established about seventeen centuries before the printing press made it possible to mass-produce books like the ones Christopher Columbus read. In some ways Alexandria's library was different from modern libraries. Its books were all written by hand. They were not bound like modern books. Instead, the texts were written on long rolls of papyrus. Papyrus was a reedy plant that grew in Egypt that was pressed into a smooth, flexible, writing material. The main library's collection included more than 490,000 papyrus rolls. Poems, plays, novels, lists, books that are in the Bible, histories, cookbooks, and more were there. Like a modern library, the books were not just stuffed on the shelves wherever there was space. They were arranged by subject and alphabetically. In building their library, the Ptolemies, the Greek kings of Egypt at that time, were dedicated collectors. They bought many books, but also collected in less straightforward ways.

Eratosthenes' own books on mathematics, geography, chronology, constellations, plays, and other subjects would have joined those on the shelves of the library. Sadly, almost none of his writing is extant. We know many of his books' titles, and some of what he said. Because lines from his works and poems were quoted by other ancients, we have a few fragments in his own words. One book that survives may be an edited version of his *Catasterisms*, about constellations. Scholars argue about its authorship.

Fortunately, other Greeks who read Eratosthenes' works wrote about him. The geographer Strabo is an especially valuable source. In Strabo's *Geography*, he quoted Eratosthenes, reproduced his map, and discussed many of his ideas. Cleomedes, another Greek scholar, wrote about Eratosthenes' measurement of the earth. Archimedes, one of the greatest mathematicians of all time, gave us glimpses of the librarian's skill and reputation for knowledge. Later Greek and Roman literature and mathematical works are peppered with references to Eratosthenes and quotes from him. These help us piece together the story of a remarkable man and his achievements. While scholars would love to have more details about Eratosthenes, a rich picture of him still emerges. We still have a sense of his influence and contributions in the ancient world.

"Another Plato," one ancient source called Eratosthenes, associating him with one of the greatest philosophers of all time. Some called him "Pentathlos," the title of an athlete who competed in the rigorous five-event competition in the Olympics. He had more than five areas of expertise, as a geographer, mathematician, historian, theater critic, chronicler of the mythology of the heavens, poet, and library administrator. Eratosthenes was also referred to as "Beta," the second letter of the Greek alphabet. Some speculate that the title may have been because he was considered second in mathematics to Archimedes and second in knowledge to Plato, but not Alpha, or first, in either category. One mathematics scholar suggested that Beta referred to his office or lecture hall in Alexandria. (Another Alexandrian, an astronomer, was known as Epsilon, the fifth Greek letter.) Eratosthenes' nickname, Beta, is sometimes seen as an intended insult by other Greeks, meaning that he was second best. Some scholars in Alexandria were very competitive and jealous of each others' successes.

Scholars today view Eratosthenes as a diverse multitalented thinker who was also "Alpha" in geography. His mathematical approach opened new ways to describe and understand the world. His work in chronology, theater criticism, and as director of the Alexandrian library made its mark in Greek thought. His ideas were among the Greeks' valuable contributions to later Western learning.

# Boy From Cyrene

CYRENE, THE CITY OF ERATOSTHENES' childhood, stood closer to the sands of the Sahara Desert than to Athens. Perched on the north coast of Africa, ancient Cyrene was located in territory that is now in the country of Libya. Although native Libyans lived in the region surrounding Eratosthenes' hometown, Cyrene was Greek. Citizens of Cyrene had Greek ancestors, spoke the Greek language, believed in Greek gods, and followed Greek customs and traditions.

Cities of the ancient Greeks were not just in the country we now call Greece. In Eratosthenes' time, Greeks had established city-states in France, on Sicily, in Turkey, in North Africa, and elsewhere. The philosopher Plato wrote that Greeks surrounded the Mediterranean Sea like frogs around a pond.

Cyrene was founded in 630 B.C. Around that time, Greeks established colonies in many places outside of the homeland. The people who settled Cyrene were from Thera, a volcanic island just north of Crete. Legend had it that the king of Thera, who stuttered, went to the sanctuary at Delphi and asked the gods to cure him of his speech impediment. A priestess there told him the gods wanted him to start a colony in Libya. King Battus, whose name means stutterer, at first delayed. Eventually, he set off with boatloads of Theran settlers. After adventures with native Libyans, Battus founded Cyrene, about ten miles (sixteen kilometers) from the coast, in green and fertile lowland hills.[1]

Ancient sources report that Eratosthenes' father was named Aglaos. They indicate that the multitalented geographer was born in about 276 B.C. Beyond that, we have no details of

Eratosthenes' youth. We do, however, know about his home and about Greek life at that time.

Cyrene in the third century B.C. was thriving. The city had grown much since Battus's time. Its homes, temples, workshops, markets, and government buildings stretched out across broad terraces on the hillside. Although sited a few miles inland, Cyrene looked over Apollonia, the city's port, to the azure Mediterranean Sea.

Temples and other religious structures were the grandest buildings in Cyrene. For ancient Greeks, belief in gods and goddesses was central to their lives. To honor these deities, the Greeks built sanctuaries with fine temples, theaters, and columned walkways. Wealthy Cyrene had spectacular buildings for the gods. The city's temple of Zeus resembled the Parthenon in Athens, but was even larger. An entire sanctuary complex, including a semicircular stone amphitheater cut into a hillside, was dedicated to Apollo. Apollo was the god of light, healing, and intellect. Cyrenaeans had a special affection for Apollo and considered him the patron god of their city.

Greek gods and goddesses would have been part of Eratosthenes' life from birth. The Greeks had a rich mythology about an extended family of immortal deities. The deities had human forms and personalities, but they also had extraordinary powers. Each god or goddess represented a different interest. Poseidon, for

The Temple of Zeus at Cyrene ressembles the Parthenon in Athens, but was even bigger.

18

example, was the god of the sea; Aphrodite was the goddess of love. Zeus was the most powerful god. He was also father to several other divinities, including Athena, patroness of the city of Athens. Beyond the twelve main deities, Greeks also believed in dozens of minor gods and heroes.

Besides building temples for them, the Greeks honored their gods through ceremonies and with gifts. Some observances took place in the privacy of homes. When a baby was born, its father carried the infant around the fire hearth three times to honor the goddess Hestia. A kindly goddess, Hestia was associated with home, hospitality, and family well-being. Other celebrations were lavish public events. The Olympics, athletic competitions held in the city of Olympia every four years, honored Zeus. The Anthesteria, a springtime festival, was dedicated to Dionysus, the god of wine. Wine was a mainstay of the Greek diet and was usually diluted with water.

A regular part of Greek festivals was animal

**Ruins of the Sanctuary of Apollo in Cyrene.**

sacrifice. Cows, oxen, goats, and other domestic animals were slaughtered by priests on special altars as offerings to the gods. In the offering ritual, the priests would sprinkle a few drops of water on the head of the living animal. Startled by the water, the creature would nod up and down. This was seen as a sign that it agreed to its sacrifice. The priest would then stun the animal and quickly kill it with a knife. In an elaborate ceremony, the sacrifices were roasted and their meat was eaten by the celebrants.[2]

Eratosthenes would have participated in these observances and feasts in Cyrene.

One aspect of Eratosthenes' youth is certain—he was well educated. Ancient Greeks had schools for boys starting at age seven. Education may have been more available for the wealthy, but there are many references to Greek schools in ancient sources. Studies covered three areas: literature, athletics, and music. Boys learned to read and write, recite poetry, and speak in public. They trained in sports, especially running and throwing.

Eratosthenes may have studied with a fellow Cyrenaean named Callimachus. Callimachus was a poet and grammarian. He became one of the intellectual leaders in Alexandria. He reportedly wrote more than eight hundred works; a few of his poems still exist. It is unclear if Eratosthenes studied with Callimachus in childhood, or as a colleague in Alexandria.

As a boy, Eratosthenes no doubt spent time in Cyrene's busy agora—the city's meeting place and commercial center. Government offices were located there as were shops and stalls selling everyday items and luxuries. Bread, wine, pottery, perfumes, textiles, and other goods traded hands in the market. Deals were made there for selling Cyrene's fine horses and citron wood, and for exporting local products. The land around Cyrene was fertile and well watered. Grains grew so abundantly there that during a devastating four-year drought in 330–326 B.C., Cyrene donated tons of wheat and barley to other Greek cities. An engraved public monument listed the cities that benefited from Cyrene's generosity.[3]

Eratosthenes would have been familiar with a plant that we will never see. Silphium grew only in a very small region right around Cyrene. The plant had a bulb at its base. Blade-like leaves grew off its central stalk. Very fragrant, silphium had many medical uses. Its juice was a treatment for aches and pains, fevers, coughs, warts, and more. Sheep and cattle apparently loved to eat silphium, and it gave their meat a pleasing flavor. Selling silphium made so much money for

Silphium, a plant that had medicinal qualities and was foraged by livestock, once grew wild around Cyrene. It was so important to Cyrene's economy that it was imprinted on their coins. Silphium is the first documented extinction of a species.

the Cyrenaeans that its image was on their coins. Harvested and sold by the Cyrenaeans and foraged by livestock, the plant became rarer and rarer. In a book about natural history written in A.D. 77, the wonders of silphium are described. The author, Pliny, also noted that it no longer existed in its natural habitat. The last known stalk of silphium was reportedly sent to the Roman emperor Nero.[4] Silphium is the first species whose extinction was documented. (Rosinweed, a North American plant with yellow flowers, now has the scientific name silphium. This is a different plant than the silphium of Cyrene.)

News of events beyond Cyrene would have reached Eratosthenes' young ears. Ships from

Greek and foreign lands docked at Apollonia. The most exciting news in the years of his youth was likely from Alexandria. Alexandria was located about five hundred miles (eight hundred kilometers) east of Cyrene and was the capital of Egypt. Greek kings of Egypt, the father Ptolemy I and his son Ptolemy II, were spending fortunes to make their city magnificent. A huge lighthouse, wide boulevards paved in granite, wild animal parks—all kinds of amazing things were turning Alexandria into an extraordinary metropolis. Eratosthenes would have heard about a new institution there, the Ptolemies' Museum.

## Athens

As a young man, Eratosthenes left Cyrene to continue his studies in Athens, the ancient version of a college education. We have the names of several Greek thinkers who may have been his teachers. Apparently some of his studies were at the Academy. The Academy was founded by the philosopher Plato about a hundred years

**The Acropolis in Athens. Eratosthenes studied and lived in Athens as a young man.**

before Eratosthenes went to Athens. Situated in a park-like grove, the Academy had a temple to the Muses, goddesses of arts and intellect.

Plato was one of the most famous philosophers of all time. His ideas and studies covered a broad range of subjects. The nature of man and laws of thought were his main interests, but he looked to arithmetic and geometry as keys to the universe. The inscription at the entrance of the Academy supposedly read, "Let none that is ignorant of geometry enter my doors."[5] Although Plato had died years before Eratosthenes was born, his Academy continued.

Teachers and ideas no doubt changed over the years. Still, at the Academy, Eratosthenes likely had considerable training in mathematics and geometry. At least one of Eratosthenes' teachers was from another of the academic traditions in Athens. Ariston of Chios was a Peripatetic.[6] The Peripatetics followed and furthered the teachings of the philosopher Aristotle. Aristotle's many studies covered subjects from marine biology to government to logic to economics.

A wedding across the Mediterranean Sea may have influenced the rest of Eratosthenes' life. Ptolemy III, who was about the same age as Eratosthenes, became king of Egypt in 246 B.C. Ptolemy III married Berenice, a princess from Cyrene. With the marriage, Cyrene became part of the Ptolemaic domain. At about the same time, Eratosthenes, who was about thirty years old, was invited by King Ptolemy III to the royal court in Alexandria.

# ALEXANDRIA

AS HE SAILED INTO ALEXANDRIA, THE first thing that Eratosthenes would have seen was the lighthouse. Standing more than 500 feet (152 meters) high, the lighthouse, called the Pharos, was one of the seven wonders of the ancient world. As tall as a modern fifty-story building, the Pharos guided approaching ships to Alexandria's fine harbor. A fire burning on its top level was reflected by a mirror so it could be seen for many miles by ships at night. The Pharos was also a tourist attraction. Visitors climbed its hundreds of steps to see breathtaking views of the city and the sea. There were even snack bars on one level selling fruit, kebabs, and drinks to visitors.[1]

The Pharos, like the palaces and other grand buildings of Alexandria, was built by the family who invited Eratosthenes to their city. The Ptolemies were one of the great dynasties of all time. A dynasty is a sequence of rulers in the

The massive Pharos lighthouse at Alexandria's harbor was one of the seven wonders of the ancient world. This artist's rendition of it is based on some of the ancient descriptions of this landmark.

same family. The Ptolemies ruled Egypt for nearly three hundred years. In the third century B.C., the first Ptolemy kings were establishing their family's fame. With the enormous wealth of Egypt in their control, they embarked on projects that supported their personal interests and also impressed rulers and peoples around them.

Alexandria was founded by Alexander the Great in 332 B.C. when he was vanquishing North Africa. Alexander, a formidable military leader, conquered lands from Greece through the Middle East, even reaching India. With his victories, he spread Greek culture and language. Alexander established a vast empire; he was its king and ruler. On his military campaigns, Alexander founded Greek cities in lands he dominated. Many were named Alexandria.

Alexander supposedly dreamed that the poet Homer directed him to the mouth of the Nile River to build his city in Egypt. After the conqueror approved this site for Alexandria, a city plan was laid out on the ground. The surveyors used flour to draw the lines. In short order, flocks of birds flew down and ate the flour. Alexander was alarmed, and believed that this was a bad omen. An oracle, a religious seer who predicted the future, said that this was actually a good omen. As the birds were fed by the flour, he said, this meant that Alexandria would be great and would feed many nations.[2]

The conqueror never got to see this namesake city. He died in 323 B.C. in Babylon at age thirty-two. Alexander's vast empire was divided after his death. One of his generals, Ptolemy I, won the prize of Egypt. Egypt was rich in grain and was the world's main source of papyrus, a plant used for making a form of paper. Selling grain and papyrus to other lands made fortunes, especially for Egypt's rulers. Taxes collected on goods that came to Egypt from other lands also fattened the royal treasury. Around 300 B.C., Ptolemy I settled into Alexandria. He set out to transform the military town into a brilliant capital. Along with Ptolemy I's grand plans, he had intellectual interests.

Ptolemy I was a historian. He wrote accounts of Alexander's military campaigns.[3]

## Museum

Ptolemy I ruled Egypt from 305 B.C. to 282 B.C. His son, Ptolemy II, followed, reigning from 282 B.C. to 246 B.C. In those six decades, father and son made Alexandria a symbol of the greatness of its founder and kings. One of their most remarkable projects was the Museum, a kind of temple dedicated to the Muses. The Greek word, which we translate as *museum*, was *mouseion*. The Muses were nine goddesses of creative and scholarly pursuits. Each Muse had a special interest: Urania was the goddess of astronomy; Clio was the Muse of history; Euterpe's specialty was music; Erato was the goddess of love poetry. Thalia and Melpomene were the Muses of comic and tragic theater, respectively; their symbols of happy and sad masks are still associated with theater. Terpsichore was the goddess of dance; her sister Polymnia was the Muse of religious hymns. Calliope was the goddess of epic poetry, like Homer's *Iliad* and *Odyssey*.

While there were other temples to these goddesses, the Museum founded by the Ptolemies was different. In Alexandria, the Muses were honored by scholars practicing the arts that the goddesses represented. To honor Melpomene, for example, experts studied plays by Euripides, Sophocles, and Aeschylus, three great tragic playwrights. They analyzed the playwrights' choices of words, studied the structure of the plays, and examined the plays' connections to Greek history.

The Museum was part of the Ptolemies' palace complex. Scholars lived, ate, and studied there in beautiful surroundings. Groves of trees, royal residences, shrines to the gods, and even a zoo were in the grounds.[4] The Museum was somewhat like a modern university, with scholars doing research and exchanging ideas.

In 2004, archaeologists announced that they found ruins under the modern city of Alexandria that may have been part of the Museum and its

One of the Muses reading a scroll is depicted on this Greek vase from 435–425 B.C.

library. They found thirteen large rooms that seemed to be lecture halls. In these spacious chambers were elevated platforms where lecturers may have stood to teach classes. The archaeologists estimated that as many as five thousand students could have studied in the spacious rooms.[5] Archaeological excavations may soon provide answers to many questions about Alexandria's library and Museum.

To attract thinkers to Alexandria, the Ptolemies paid scholars to come to their Museum. Food, lodging, and even spending money were granted to them. With this generous royal arrangement, thinkers came. Zenodotus, an expert in Homer's poetry, was one of the first. In Alexandria, Zenodotus studied many versions of the *Iliad* and the *Odyssey*. He edited them to create an official edition, as close as possible to what he believed were Homer's originals. Zenodotus also developed an alphabetically arranged glossary of unusual Greek words, like a dictionary. Zenodotus became the first director of the library.

The mathematician Euclid was another early arrival in Alexandria. His comprehensive multivolume work *The Elements* laid out propositions and proofs in geometry. It is the basis for teaching geometry even today. King Ptolemy I reportedly asked Euclid if there was an easier way to learn the subject than to study *The Elements*. Euclid famously replied, "There is no royal road to geometry."[6] Even though he was a king, Euclid was saying, Ptolemy would have to work through the logical steps of geometry just like everyone else.

Writers, historians, physicians, and scholars studying nature and the laws of physics flocked to Alexandria's Museum. Intellectually, it was a sparkling center of Greek thought.

## The Library

The first two Ptolemies bestowed another incomparable gift on the scholars. Along with the Museum, they established a library. Private collections of writings had existed before, but this collection was not just for the use of its owner. This was truly a library, whose books and knowledge were open to many. The Ptolemies developed it with vigor. By the time Eratosthenes arrived in their city, the library held thousands upon thousands of Greek volumes.

Homer's epics were on the library shelves— several versions of them. Hundreds of Greek plays were there, including more than seventy by Aeschylus. Today, only six of Aeschylus's works still exist. Medical texts, political speeches, historical accounts, cookbooks, mathematical tracts, and more were in the collection. Books of lists were there—including volumes that listed the seven wonders of the ancient world. (Alexandria's own lighthouse was on that list, along with the pyramids and other spectacular sites.) Philosophy was well represented, with works by incomparable thinkers like Plato and Aristotle. The library also held work by non-Greeks, translated into the Greek language. Egyptian histories and lists of pharaohs were there. Jewish scriptures were translated from

Hebrew and Aramaic into Greek for the collection.[7]

Over 490,000 papyrus rolls of texts were in Alexandria's main library. A second "daughter" library housed another 42,800 rolls.[8] It is not known how many individual books this represented, because some books took up several rolls and there were multiple copies of some.

To understand the significance of this lost library, we can take a brief look at factors that led to its creation. Greeks had a written language before 1400 B.C. In their earliest writing, they used symbols for syllables. One early Greek script is now known as Linear B. During the so-called Greek dark age, from the 1100s B.C., this form of writing seems to have died out. It remained dead for a long time. For centuries, no one knew the meaning of its little symbols. With determination and clever detective work, scholars finally deciphered Linear B in the 1950s.

Around 800 B.C., ancient Greeks started writing again, but in a different way. Instead of the syllable symbols they had used earlier, they borrowed letters used by Phoenicians, and adapted a Greek phonetic alphabet. Using about two dozen symbols representing different sounds, they could write all of the words of their language.[9] The word "alphabet" is a blend of their first two letters, alpha and beta.

Greeks had long and rich traditions of poetry and public speaking. Homer's *Iliad* and *Odyssey* and other works, composed before widespread literacy, were originally spoken. People memorized these poems and recited them like songs. Through centuries they were passed on through an oral tradition. When the Greeks resumed reading and writing with their new phonetic alphabet, they no longer depended on word of mouth. Reading and writing were powerful tools for communication and sharing knowledge. From Greek art and documents, it seems that literacy was spreading quickly around 500 B.C.[10] Scenes decorating vases from that time show readers with open rolls with letters written on them.

In the fifth century B.C., schools were

teaching reading and writing to boys who were students. Writing was rapidly becoming part of daily life. For example, citizens scratched names of statesmen on broken pottery pieces to vote for them in elections. Written records were kept of taxes and public projects, including building costs for the temples on the acropolis in Athens. Government decrees were inscribed on stone monuments. Works that were previously spoken were transcribed. A person could read Homer's *Iliad* from a written copy rather than learning it by ear.

A product from Egypt helped spread literacy and the rise of written books. Papyrus is a reed that grows in Egypt. Since about 3,000 B.C., Egyptians manufactured a kind of paper from it. The word "paper" is derived from papyrus.

To make paper, Egyptians harvested stalks of papyrus. They laid several long stalks side by side. Across these they placed a layer of shorter stalks. This crisscrossed mat was then pressed with a heavy weight that squeezed the reeds together. Papyrus juices glued the layers and

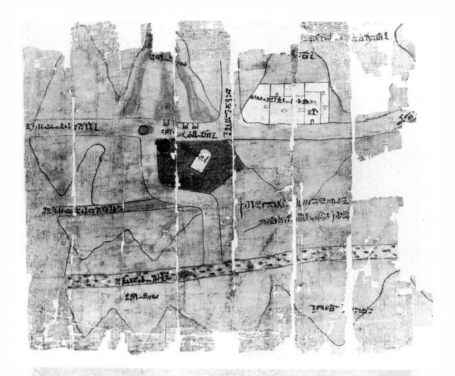

Egyptians made a form of paper from papyrus reeds. This 1300s B.C map showing locations of Egyptian gold mines is on papyrus. The texts of the Alexandrian library were written on rolls of papyrus.

stalks together. When the weight was removed, the resulting paper was smooth and flexible. Egyptians typically glued several papyrus sheets together. The combined sheets could be more than ten feet (three meters) long. Papyrus sheets could crack if folded, but they could easily be rolled and unrolled. Tax receipts, government forms, or letters often required only small pieces of papyrus; long works were recorded on multiple rolls.

Papyrus was well suited to Egypt in many ways. Not only did the plant thrive there, but manufactured papyrus could last a long time in Egypt's hot dry climate. Papyrus is organic; in a damp environment it molds and rots. In Egypt, however, it was durable. Hundreds of thousands of papyrus fragments with ancient writings have been recovered from the desert sands.

## Eratosthenes the Librarian

Eratosthenes was reportedly invited by the king, probably Ptolemy III, to Alexandria in about 245 B.C. He was in his thirties and had likely already established his reputation as a thinker in Athens. Callimachus, who was also from Cyrene, was already in Alexandria and achieving considerable fame. Callimachus had been a teacher. His poetry and scholarship, though, were his lasting achievements. Best known today for his poems, Callimachus had broad interests. *On Birds, On Winds, Customs of Barbarians*, and the intriguing *On Changes of Names in Fish* are among his book titles.[11] He also wrote the authoritative *Tables of persons eminent in every branch of learning, together with a list of their writings*. This lengthy tome, with one hundred twenty different subject sections, was called *Tables* for short.[12] *Tables* was a list of writers and all significant written Greek works of the time. The Ptolemies either had or wanted to have all of these writings in their library.

There is some confusion about the earliest directors of Alexandria's library. Eratosthenes was perhaps the third man to hold that position. This was a royal appointment; the librarian worked for the king. Some library directors were also tutors to the king's children. It is not known if teaching royal teens was among Eratosthenes' duties.

We are not certain what Alexandria's library looked like. Ancient descriptions and later libraries offer clues. A long row of columns probably ran down one side of the building. A roof supported by the columns would have shaded a wide porch-like space. From the porch, doorways probably opened into individual library rooms. In these rooms, rolls of papyrus texts were stored on shelves in leather or pottery holders. Scholars could take the rolls out to study in the natural light of the porch. From ancient descriptions, it seems that the library was attached to the Museum.

The director of Alexandria's library oversaw its operation, including acquiring new books. The Ptolemies were voracious book collectors. The two main book markets of the day were in Athens and on the island of Rhodes. Alexandrian agents frequented both of these markets, buying new titles and copies of classics. The Ptolemies also had a policy of seizing books from ships that came to Alexandria. On arrival, ships in the port were searched. Books found on board were confiscated. They were then copied by library scribes and the copies returned to the ships.

A famous book deal occurred during

Eratosthenes' time as librarian. The city of Athens had official copies of plays by three of its greatest playwrights: Euripides, Sophocles, and Aeschylus. All three had lived around two hundred years before Eratosthenes. Over the years different directors and actors had altered the plays. The Athenians were displeased that these treasures of the theater had been changed. To preserve the genius of the playwrights, Athens had certified official versions of the plays. These versions were believed to be in the playwrights' original words. Ptolemy III wanted those originals. The Athenians only agreed to loan the plays if the king would put up a huge amount of money to guarantee their return. Ptolemy III gave the Athenians fifteen gold talents (unit of weight of gold) that they requested. With the originals in his possession, he had the plays copied on the finest quality papyrus. Then he gave the Athenians the copies and forfeited the gold. The prized originals stayed in Alexandria.[13]

When books arrived in Alexandria for the

library, first they went to warehouses for sorting and cataloguing. Each one was labeled with its source, author, and subject. Volumes taken from visiting sailors were labeled "from the ships." The library would have had a scriptorium, a place where books were copied. We know nothing about the identities of scribes or other workers in the library. It is likely that they were slaves, as were many other workers in the ancient Greek world.[14]

Eratosthenes served as library director from about 245 B.C. to about 200 B.C. His talents and interests left their mark on the library's scholarship. Mathematical and scientific interests particularly flourished during his tenure. Archimedes, the brilliant mathematician who stated the law of the lever and the principle of buoyancy, had strong ties to the library during Eratosthenes' years. Archimedes lived in Syracuse, a city on the island of Sicily. He spent some time in Alexandria, though. Even after he had returned to his homeland, he sent his mathematical and scientific writing to the library.

Other mathematicians including Conon and Dositheus were also at the Museum at that time.

Eratosthenes drew on the library's vast resources to further learning through his own projects and texts. From accounts of Alexander the Great's campaigns and reports from trading expeditions, he developed a map of the world. From works by Euclid, Archimedes, and others, he solved challenging mathematical problems, including how to double a cube. Sifting through hundreds of jumbled accounts of events in the Greek past, he figured out dates when they had occurred. His chronology ordered historic events from the fall of Troy to the death of Alexander the Great. From poems and other writings, he found the myths associated with constellations seen in the night sky. He then compiled the stories that explained how those figures were placed in the heavens. Combining his mathematical knowledge and accounts of astronomical observations, he measured the circumference of the earth.

# 4

# MEASURING THE EARTH

HOW COULD AN ANCIENT GREEK MEASURE the earth? Eratosthenes traveled from Cyrene to Athens to Alexandria, but probably never went more than a thousand miles from his home. Yet, he was able to calculate the size of our globe with surprising accuracy.

Eratosthenes and other ancient Greeks knew that the earth was round. Their personal observations showed them that its surface was curved. Respected thinkers wrote and taught about the spherical earth. The philosopher Aristotle, in particular, offered compelling evidence of the planet's shape.

Ancient Greeks were seafaring people. Their ships with oars and sails traveled between islands and across the Mediterranean Sea. For sailors, the curvature of the earth's surface was obvious. They saw it as they sailed from ports with tall buildings or past islands with high cliffs. Leaving Alexandria with its Pharos lighthouse, sailors saw the full height of the lighthouse when close to it. When they were a few miles away, they lost sight of the bottom of the structure. At a greater distance, only the top of the lighthouse with its reflected flame was visible. Farther out at sea, that too slipped down out of sight. The same phenomenon was seen by people on land watching ships sail away. In the distance, ships' hulls disappeared first below the horizon. Gradually their masts would slide down and disappear. The earth's curved surface explained this phenomenon.

More than three hundred years before Eratosthenes, philosophers were offering their views of the shape of the earth. Some thought it was a disk. Pythagoras, a mathematician and philosopher from the island of Samos, claimed that the earth was a sphere. The sun and moon moved around it in circular paths, he suggested.

In the fourth century B.C., Aristotle offered his evidence of the spherical shape of the earth. In lunar eclipses, Aristotle noted, the earth's round shadow was seen gliding across the face of the full moon. The variation of stars' elevations above the horizon when viewed from more northerly or southerly locations also revealed the earth's curved surface and spherical shape, he said.

The philosopher Aristotle noted that ancient Greeks saw the curvature of Earth as they saw ships "hull down." As seen from a tower, a ship's hull disappears before the top of its main mast. This image is from a book printed in 1585, as Europeans were rediscovering Greek ideas and learning.

PRIMVS. 25

altissima montium cacumina, & profundissimæ valles ostendat nobis terram multis in locis nõ esse perfecte sphæricã: hæc tamẽ nullius momẽti sunt. quia respectu maximæ quãtitatis totius globi terræ & aquæ altissimi montes, profundissimẽq; valles, tãquã imperceptibilia pũcta existũt. inftar Mali Medici,qd licet paruulas habeat emi nẽtias, nihilominus sphæricũ eft. & fimiliter maximẽ planities respectu magnitudinis globi terræ,& aquæ, licet oculis noftris planæ videantur, nihilofecius sphæricæ sũt. Si quis enim ex circûfe rẽtia cuiufpiã maximẽ quãtitatis circuli exiguam admodũ parte abfcinderet, dubio procul à quoli bet illa particula feorsũ afpecta, recta linea esse iu dicaretur.idẽ aũt euenit etiã de maximæ fphæræ fuperficie.Quòd verò iã dictæ vifui apparẽtes ter ræ planities, & mariũ amplifsimæ fupficies, fphæ ricæ fint, hinc etiã cõfirmatur. ç cùm in ipfis ter ræ maximis apparẽtibus planitiebus verfus remo tifsimos à nobis mõtes peragramus, aut litoraver fus nauigamus,ipfa mõtiũ cacumina quafi è ma ri,terraq; emergẽtia furgere,corũq; magnitudo paulatim crefcere nobis vidẽt cùm antea propter globi ter ræ, & a quæ ro tundita tẽ latuif fent. vt fe ques figu ra de monftrar.

Exemplũ pul cherrimum.

Alia ratio probans ter ræ, & aquæ fu perficie fphæ ricam esse.

Figuraofiẽ dens glo bum terræ & aquẽ ef fe fphæri cum.

Idem

49

26    LIBER

Alia ratio idem probis. Idē autē hac etiam ratione cōprobatur. Quia si sit in litore maris signum aliquod, vt ædificium, vel quæuis alia res eminens, nauisque ab ipso litore discedat, tantumq; recedat, quod oculus eius, qui stat in pede Mali, nopossit signum illud videre : naui manente oculus eiusdem stantis in summitate Mali signum illud optimē videbit. attamen melius deberet illud cernere oculus eius, qui stat iuxta pedem Mali (cùm illud per breuiorem lineam videat) quàm oculus eius, qui supra Mali summitatem ascendit, quippe qui longiori linea, siue radio visuali illud videt. quemadmodū Geometris, ac perspectiuis manifestum est per rectas lineas ductas, aut excogitatas ab ambobus dictis locis ad illud signum : cuius quidem rei nulla alia est causa, quàm aquæ rotūditas, remotis (inquam) omnibus alijs impedimentis, quæ accidentaliter contingere possunt ; vt sunt nubes, vapores ascendentes, aliaq; idgenus. vt ostendit sequens figura.

*Figura idem ostendens.*

Similiter

The top of a tower was visible to ships at sea before they could see the land beneath it, also showing Earth's curved surface.

"For if we make a slight change of position northward or southward, the horizon visibly changes, so that the stars above our head change greatly," wrote Aristotle. He continued, "Some stars are observed in Egypt and about Cyprus, but are not observed in the regions towards the north, and those stars seen continuously in the northern regions set in these regions. In consequence, not only is it clear from this that earth's shape is round, but also that it has the shape of a sphere of no great size, since it would not make it obvious so quickly when we change our positions by so little."[1] Aristotle also noted that "mathematicians who attempt to reckon up the size of the circumference say that it approaches four hundred thousand stades."[2] He neglected to say how they found that figure.

## Measuring Earth

Eratosthenes' most famous achievement was likely laid out in his book titled *On the Measurement of the Earth*. Regrettably, like almost

The philosopher Aristotle argued that Earth was shaped like a sphere. As evidence, he observed that during a lunar eclipse, when Earth passes directly between the sun and the moon, Earth's round shadow can be seen on the face of the moon.

all of his writing, it no longer exists. Our information about Eratosthenes' method and measurement comes from later sources. Strabo, a geographer who lived about two centuries after Eratosthenes, recorded Eratosthenes' result—but not how he found it. Cleomedes, who was probably a teacher, wrote a treatise titled *The Heavens*. This astronomical handbook included a brief, straightforward account of Eratosthenes' procedure. We have no facts about Cleomedes' life, but scholars estimate that his book was composed sometime between 50 B.C. and A.D. 200.[3]

Eratosthenes' genius in measuring the earth was in bringing together simple observations and basic mathematical concepts. "His introduction of the principles of mathematics and physics into the subject is a commendable thing," wrote Strabo.[4]

To understand Eratosthenes' approach we can start with assumptions he made and knowledge he had. First Eratosthenes assumed that the earth was a perfect sphere, even though its surface was irregular with mountains and oceans. (It is not actually perfectly spherical, it bulges a bit at the equator.) He also assumed that the sun was so far away from the earth that its rays of light could be considered parallel to each other anywhere on the earth.[5] In this, he was correct. This assumption allowed him to use his knowledge of a basic rule of geometry for his calculation. This rule was laid out in Euclid's *The Elements*, a geometry book that was one of the classics of Alexandrian scholarship. Euclid had shown that if two parallel lines are crossed by a third line, the alternate interior angles are equal. The alternate interior angles are inside the parallel lines and on alternate sides of the transverse (see diagram).

"Eratosthenes says, and it is the case, that Syene is located below the summer tropical circle. So when the sun . . . produces the summer solstice . . . the pointers on the sundials are necessarily shadowless, since the sun is located vertically above them," explained Cleomedes.[6] Eratosthenes had learned that on the summer

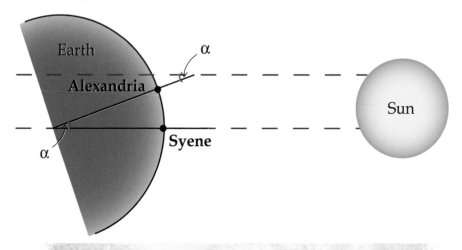

Eratosthenes measured the circumference of Earth by using mathematics and observation. He correctly assumed that the sun was so far from Earth its rays striking Earth could be considered parallel lines. From geometry he knew that when two parallel lines are crossed by a third straight line, the alternate interior angles are equal.

solstice, the sun passed directly overhead in the town of Syene. The summer solstice, or June solstice, occurs each year in the Northern Hemisphere when the tilt of the earth's axis is oriented most toward the sun. On this day, the sun makes its most northerly annual pass through the sky. Syene stood about five hundred miles (eight hundred kilometers) south of Alexandria on the Nile River.

It is sometimes said that Eratosthenes knew of a well in Syene that the sun shone into on the solstice. This well was not mentioned by Cleomedes. Strabo wrote about it, but not in connection with Eratosthenes. "In Syene is also the well that marks the summer tropic," wrote Strabo. "It is at Syene that the sun first gets over our heads and causes the gnomons [sundials] to cast no shadow at midday; and necessarily, when the sun gets over our heads, it also casts its rays into wells as far as the water, even if they are very deep; for we ourselves stand perpendicular to the earth and wells are dug perpendicular to the surface."[7] One can envision the noonday sun directly overhead, with its rays illuminating water at the bottom of a well.

Eratosthenes knew that the sun was never directly overhead in Alexandria. At its highest point in the sky on the summer solstice, it was still slightly in the southern sky. Cleomedes noted that "in Alexandria at the same hour pointers on sundials do cast a shadow, since this city is located further north than Syene."[8] For his calculation, Eratosthenes needed to determine the angle between vertical and the sun's position over Alexandria at noon on the solstice. Another way of understanding this is as the angle of the sun's rays striking Alexandria.

To find this measurement, Eratosthenes likely used a sundial. One type of sundial is a scaphe. A scaphe is a hemispherical bowl with a gnomon in its center. The gnomon is a vertical stick of the same radius as the sphere. It stands at the lowest point of the bowl. The shadow of the gnomon can be measured against curves inscribed inside the bowl.

Eratosthenes found that the shadow cast by the gnomon from the sun's rays at the sun's highest point in the sky was equal to 1/50 of a full circle.[9] Geometry then answered one of his questions. Remember that the sun's rays striking Alexandria were parallel to the sun's rays striking Syene at the same time. At Syene, as the sun passed overhead, an imaginary line could be drawn from the sun through Syene, straight to the center of the earth. The line from the sun through Alexandria would not pass through the earth's center. However, a line could be drawn through the gnomon, which stood vertical at the earth's surface, right through the planet's center. Inside the intersection of this line and the Syene line would be the alternate interior angle of the shadow's angle. As the gnomon's angle was 1/50 of a circle, this angle was also 1/50 of a circle. Carrying that angle back to the earth's surface, the distance between Syene and Alexandria would also be 1/50 of the earth's circumference.

To finish the problem, Eratosthenes needed to know the distance between Syene and Alexandria. Eratosthenes believed this distance to be five thousand stades. A stade was an ancient measure of length. No one knows how this measurement was made. It may have been an estimate based on travel time. Possibly it was measured by men walking with even paces on straight sections of a line between the two cities.[10]

If 5,000 stades was equal to one-fiftieth of the distance around the earth, then 250,000 stades was equal to the whole circle—the circumference of the earth. After determining that number, Eratosthenes apparently made an adjustment. He rounded it up to 252,000 stades. Today this seems a curious move, but Eratosthenes had a reason. Much of ancient Greek astronomy and observation was tied to Babylonian traditions. The Babylonians used a number system based on 60. This system still shows in our modern world with 360 degrees in a circle. 252,000 divided by 60 equals 4,200, a less cumbersome number for calculations than 250,000 divided by 60.

One major question about Eratosthenes' measurement is the size of the stade that he used. Using a common Egyptian measurement, a stade was 517 feet (158 meters), yielding a circumference of 24,663 miles (39,691 kilometers). That measurement is impressively close to the modern measurement of the equatorial circumference of 24,902 miles (40,075 kilometers). Some scholars suggest that he may have used a longer Olympic stade of 586 feet (179 meters). Even by this measurement, Eratosthenes would have missed by only about three thousand miles (forty-eight hundred kilometers).

Careful examination of Eratosthenes' assumptions and measurements reveals a couple of little flaws. In fact, Syene is slightly farther north than Eratosthenes believed, so the sun was not exactly overhead. Using an Egyptian stade, the distance between the two cities was actually a bit shorter than the assumed five thousand stades. However, these errors canceled each other out to yield a remarkable result.[11]

## More Than Earth

While Eratosthenes' astonishing circumference calculation is his most famous achievement in *On the Measurement of the Earth*, this text also contained further studies of the earth and the heavens. It is believed that it included his work in astronomy as well as his measurements of distances from the earth to the sun and moon. Eratosthenes reportedly calculated timing of eclipses; his system for those may have been in this book.[12] This book may also have included his calculation of what we now call the tilt of the earth's axis.

To the ancient Greeks, the earth was not a planet revolving around the sun. Instead, they believed that the sun, moon, planets, and stars revolved around the earth. They observed the sun passing through the sky in the course of the year on a tilted path. In summer, the sun was much higher in the sky than in winter. In Syene, for example, the sun was overhead on the summer solstice. In midwinter, on the shortest day of the year, the sun did not quite reach the midway point between the horizon and its summer elevation. (The difference between these two points is about 47 degrees.)

This phenomenon of the sun's apparent annual travels is explained by the tilt of the earth's axis relative to the path it follows as it revolves around the sun. Today, we know that the earth rotates on its axis, completing one rotation each day. The earth also revolves around the sun, completing one revolution every 365 1/4 days. The earth's axial tilt does not change through the year, but our planet's position in its orbital path is always changing. For part of the year, the Northern Hemisphere points toward the sun. Gradually the earth moves into a position where the Southern Hemisphere gets more sun; then the pattern repeats.

Eratosthenes was among the first to measure the angle of the observed shift in the sun's path. He determined that it was the rather odd ratio of 11/83 of a semicircle.[13] We do not know his method, but again, he arrived at a figure of great accuracy. His calculation converts to a measurement of 23 ° 51'. Today we measure this angle, which is the same whether it is regarded as the observed tilt of the sun's path or the tilt of the earth's axis, as around 23° 26'.

# GEOGRAPHY

ERATOSTHENES HAD A LOFTY GOAL WHEN he wrote one of his major works. He called it *Geographica*, Greek for "Geography." He was the first person known to use that word. Geography comes from two ancient Greek roots. *Geo* means earth. *Graph* means to write or describe. In *Geographica*, Eratosthenes set out to describe the world. He wrote about the land from an arctic island called Thule to southern Africa and from the ocean west of the Strait of Gibraltar to the ocean east of India. He described mountains, animals, plants, and the flow of rivers. Eratosthenes wrote about the inhabited world, not just where Greeks lived, but the lands of non-Greeks, too. He also drew his image of the land of this round earth on a flat plane—a map that was the basis of centuries of maps to come.

Geography is defined by *Webster's New World Dictionary* as "the descriptive science dealing with the surface of the earth, its division into continents and countries, and the climate, plants, animals, natural resources, inhabitants, and industries of the various divisions." Modern geographers study populations, lands and oceans, and how the planet's resources can continue to sustain humankind. Geographers map ocean floors, advise companies on good locations for stores, and help communities plan for future growth. Geography is a broad science with branches that deal with many aspects of the natural and human world.

Besides coming up with a fitting name for a study of the earth, Eratosthenes played a key role in advancing that study. He laid out the basics of a system for mapping that was later refined into the longitude and latitude that we know today.[1] Eratosthenes moved the study of the earth away from myths and legends. For his description of the earth, he looked to accounts from travelers and military expeditions. When available, he used astronomical observations. Observations like the position of the solstice sun at Syene helped him to identify locations of places on the spherical earth.

## Earlier Geography

Although he coined the word "geography," Eratosthenes was not the first geographer. Since early times, people had described locations of hunting grounds, fishing streams, and places of shelter. Sumerians, ancient people of the Middle East, had maps as early as 2100 B.C.[2] An Egyptian map from around 1300 B.C. shows the Nile River, landmarks, roads, and locations of gold and silver mines (see map p. 40). In the ancient world there were many maps that showed parts of the world, stars in the sky, or plans of cities.

Greeks had been describing their world for centuries before Eratosthenes. Homer's poems told of the legendary Trojan War and the hero

Odysseus's years of wanderings on his way home. During Odysseus's long voyage, his adventures included life-threatening encounters in the land of the lotus-eaters, on the island of the one-eyed Cyclops, and on the isle of the king of the winds. These poems were considered history; ancient Greeks thought the places and people in them were founded in fact. In the fifth century B.C., the historian Herodotus wrote about Greek wars. Along with battlefields and politics, his beautifully written history informed his readers about distant lands and exotic customs. He traveled widely, visiting Eratosthenes' hometown of Cyrene as well as Egypt, the Middle East, and lands now in present-day Turkey and Italy.

The Greeks' known world was vastly expanded by Alexander the Great. His military campaigns extended through Iran and Afghanistan to India, through Babylon, and into Egypt. Some generals, like Ptolemy I, who traveled with Alexander, wrote accounts of these campaigns. They described the distances that they marched, the lands they crossed, and the people they encountered.

## Other Sources

Knowledge of new places did not just come from military expeditions. A Greek navigator named Pythias, from the city that is now Marseilles, France, traveled widely in the fourth century B.C. He sailed west through the Strait of Gibraltar, and up the coast of Europe. Pythias met people in Great Britain who built barns and drank mead, made from honey and water. Farther north, he saw a sea of ice.[3] Pythias wrote about these remarkable, unfamiliar sights.

Homer's poems and Herodotus's history, as well as the recent reports from Alexander's campaigns and Pythias's explorations, were among the texts in Alexandria's library. Eratosthenes learned about places from "the testimony of the men who had been in the regions, for he has read many historical treatises—with which he was well supplied," wrote the Greek man of letters, Strabo.[4] Strabo is our leading source of information about Eratosthenes' geography.

## Strabo

Strabo was born in Amasia, a Greek city in present-day Turkey, in about 64 B.C. He studied in Rome as a young man, and traveled extensively. His seventeen-volume *Geography* is one of the most important geographical works that we have today from the ancient world. Probably written between 9 B.C. and A.D. 5, it is very descriptive.[5] Villagers in the Alps, the iron jewelry of women in Iberia, and exceptionally large hogs raised in Belgium were among the thousands of subjects he touched on in his text. Strabo's *Geography* still offers engaging stories of foreign places in ancient times.

Strabo was an enthusiastic fan of Eratosthenes—in most areas.[6] In a way, Strabo was updating Eratosthenes' work. He saw a need to correct the mistakes of geographers before him. "And if I shall, on occasion, be compelled to contradict the very men whom in all other

Strabo, first century B.C. Greek geographer. In his own seventeen-volume *Geography*, Strabo gave a great deal of information about Eratosthenes' *Geographia*.

respects I follow most closely, I beg to be pardoned," he politely wrote.[7] Eratosthenes had expanded geography through knowledge of Alexander's campaigns, Strabo noted. By Strabo's time, there was even more knowledge of the world. Much new information had come with the expansion of the Roman Empire.

From Strabo, we know that Eratosthenes' *Geographica* included three volumes. The first one apparently dealt with background of geographic thought, including his ideas about the poet Homer. In this volume, he discussed the irregular surface of the earth, with its mountains, seas, rivers, and other physical features. He even commented on fossils like mussel and scallop shells found in the desert. Eratosthenes' second volume dealt with the length and breadth of the inhabited world—lands where people lived. Eratosthenes' map was presented in his final volume.

The deepest disagreement between Strabo and Eratosthenes was about geography as described by Homer in the *Odyssey* and the *Iliad*.

Many Greeks accepted Homer's poems, including the gods and mythological monsters, as history. They believed that the places where Odysseus met the Cyclops and others were real locations. In the first volume of *Geographica*, Eratosthenes argued that Homer was not a valid source of geographic facts. "Eratosthenes," Strabo wrote, "contends that the aim of every poet is to entertain, not to instruct."[8] According to Eratosthenes, Homer was just telling a good story. Poets, in his view, were not writing history or accurately describing lands. Strabo heartily disagreed. "Eratosthenes makes many mistakes when he speaks of these wanderings and declares that not only the commentators on Homer but Homer himself are dealers in nonsense," he countered.[9] Indignantly, Strabo directly addressed Eratosthenes, who had already been dead for almost two hundred years. "You are wrong when you deny to Homer the possession of vast learning, and go on to declare that poetry is a fable-prating old wife, who has been permitted to 'invent' (as you call it) whatever she deems suitable for purposes of entertainment."[10] From Strabo's vigorous defense of Homer, we see that Eratosthenes was moving the study of the earth away from legends. Instead he wanted it based on experiences and observations.

In Eratosthenes' second volume, he dealt with the layout of the inhabited world. Piecing together different accounts from travelers, he tried to deduce reasonable estimates of distances.[11] He used geometry, especially measurements of triangles, to try to determine locations for distant cities and landmarks. He seems to have a practical attitude about the accuracy of his sources, recognizing that reports of distances armies marched or sights they saw were imprecise. Strabo wrote that he noted some distances, "roughly speaking."[12] Adding together information he had, Eratosthenes estimated that the inhabited earth was about 77,800 stades from east to west, and about 38,000 stades from Thule to the southern extreme of inhabited land. Of course,

Eratosthenes only knew of lands in Europe, Africa, and Asia. Still, his measurement was far from accurate.

Traditionally, Greeks had mapped the world as an almost circular mass of land surrounded by ocean. The sanctuary of Delphi, the most important Greek religious site, was at its center. Eratosthenes' map, laid out in his third volume, did not follow that plan. Instead, his map used fixed points—cities, islands, and coastlines and other features. On the map he set up a base line. This line ran from the Strait of Gibraltar in the west, through the island of Rhodes (north of Alexandria) through Asia Minor, continuing past the coast of India in the east. A meridian line ran from the north, through the arctic island called Thule, crossed the base line at a right angle at Rhodes, then continued south through Alexandria, and to Syene, and to the edge of Africa.

Eratosthenes tried to relate locations of other places to these two lines. For example, he believed the southern tip of India to be at about the same latitude as Meroe, a settlement far south of Alexandria. On his map, he put the two points at the same distance south of his base line.[13] Unfortunately, few details of Eratosthenes' references and descriptions were repeated by Strabo.

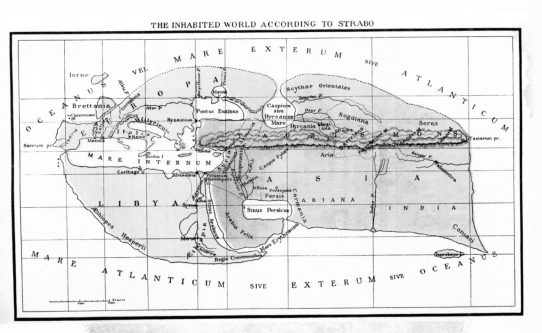

THE INHABITED WORLD ACCORDING TO STRABO

Strabo's map of the world was a later development of Eratosthenes' map. Eratosthenes did not have the lines of longitude and latitude shown on Stabo's. Instead he had one east-west base line and one north-south meridian. These intersected at Rhodes, as shown here, just east of the Greek peninsula, in the northern Mediterranean Sea.

Other features of Eratosthenes' cartography that are lost to us are his "seals." Apparently, he divided the inhabited world into several sections that related back to the larger map. The seals were like irregularly shaped regional maps. With the seals he apparently included a potpourri of information about geographic features, people, and nature of the regions.

Regarding the people of different lands, Eratosthenes disagreed with the traditional view that humanity could be divided into Greeks and Barbarians. The word *barbarian* comes from Greek, and meant uncivilized people, people who did not speak Greek. Other languages supposedly sounded to the refined Greeks like "barbar." According to Strabo, Eratosthenes argued "that it would be better to make such divisions according to good qualities and bad qualities; for not only are many of the Greeks bad, but many of the Barbarians are refined— Indians and Arians, for example, and, further, Romans and Carthaginians who carry on their governments so admirably."[14]

Eratosthenes is sometimes credited with establishing longitude and latitude. The base lines for his map helped set the stage for their later development, but these were not among his many accomplishments. Likewise, he was not the originator of climate zones defined by latitude. On this point, though, he knew the contrasts between northern frigid regions and the blazing heat of equatorial lands. In his poem titled *Hermes*, he wrote about the view of the earth seen from the heavens. He described ice at the north and south poles and a scorched, uninhabitable band at the equator.[15]

It is indeed unfortunate that we cannot read Eratosthenes' own words describing the earth. Strabo gives us just enough to know that *Geographica* was a fascinating, comprehensive, and open-minded look at the world.

# 6

## MATHEMATICIAN

ONE DAY IN THE LATE THIRD CENTURY B.C., a letter arrived in Alexandria. On a long sheet of papyrus, the letter was written in the Greek dialect spoken on the island of Sicily. "Archimedes to Eratosthenes Greeting!" the letter began. "On an earlier occasion I had sent you some theorems found by me," Archimedes wrote. In a lengthy document following the letter, he explained the steps he used to prove that those theorems were true.

"I know that you are diligent, an excellent teacher of philosophy, and greatly interested in any mathematical investigations that may come your way," Archimedes wrote to Eratosthenes.[1] The manuscript sent by Archimedes to

Eratosthenes is now known as *The Method*. It broke new ground in mathematics and is still studied today.

Archimedes was a friend of Eratosthenes and is widely regarded as one of the greatest mathematicians of all time. He articulated the law of the lever, calculated a value for pi, and discovered Archimedes' Principle of Buoyancy. Among his many achievements, he was especially proud of his discovery of relationships between cylinders and spheres. Archimedes found and proved that the volume of a sphere is 2/3 that of the circumscribed cylinder. The same proportion, he discovered, also applied to their relative surface areas. A cylinder, sphere, and Archimedes' formula were engraved on a monument at his grave.

Archimedes lived in Syracuse, on the island of Sicily, but studied in Alexandria. Even after he returned home, he sent his mathematical treatises to Alexandria. There, his work would be copied and kept in the library's collection. It could also be discussed and built upon by

Eratosthenes and other mathematicians at the Museum. In the letter with *The Method* and a note accompanying the perplexing *Cattle Problem*, we see Archimedes' respect for Eratosthenes.

Eratosthenes wrote two books about mathematics. One was titled *On Means*. We know nothing of its contents other than that it dealt with geometry. In mathematics, means are averages of terms or of quantities. A later prominent mathematician listed *On Means* along with Euclid's *Elements*, indicating that it was a well-respected text.[2] His second book, *Platonicus*, apparently dealt with the mathematics of Plato's philosophy. From a few fragments of it that still exist, it seems that it dealt with proportions and musical scales.[3] These were topics of great interest to mathematically minded ancient Greeks. Ancient Greeks knew that stretched strings produced different musical notes depending on their lengths. Different length strings played together produced harmonies. The mathematical relationships that produced these harmonies intrigued the Greeks.

Eratosthenes was among the Greeks who laid the foundation for later mathematics. Certainly, though, Greeks were not the world's first mathematicians. People in cultures long before them had ways of counting, adding and using numbers. Ancient Egyptians and Babylonians had particularly advanced mathematics. Egyptians used geometry to survey plots of land and design structures. Babylonians used mathematics for measuring, astronomical observations, and even algebra. Babylonians gave us the 360-degree circle and the twenty-four-hour day.

In the hands of the Greeks, mathematics moved in a new direction. Instead of just observing mathematical phenomena, they began asking why different aspects of mathematics were true.[4] Questioning and searching for rational answers was key to much ancient Greek thought. Their mathematics, philosophy, and science were all related.

The Greeks had a number system that we would find difficult. Numbers were represented by letters. There was no symbol for zero. Decimals did not exist. The highest number symbol was a myriad, representing ten thousand. This must have been especially cumbersome for Eratosthenes and his calculations of distances to the sun and moon.

Greek contributions to arithmetic ranged from simple concepts like even and odd numbers to identifying complex mathematical relationships. The Pythagorean Theorem is one example. This theorem expresses the relationship between the length of sides of a right triangle. It is true regardless of the size of the right triangle or the length of its sides. It can be irrefutably proven through logical steps. The Pythagorean theorem is expressed $a^2 + b^2 = c^2$, with $a$ and $b$ the legs of the triangle, and $c$ the hypotenuse.

In Alexandria, mathematical thought flourished. Mathematicians met there and studied each other's works. They discussed problems and examined their colleagues' analyses. Through exchange of ideas and access to texts,

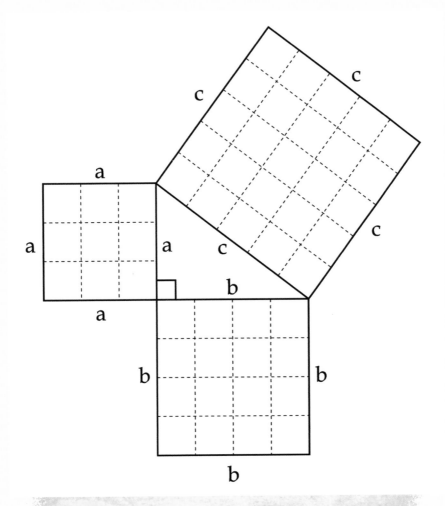

The Pythagorean Theorem states that the sum of the squares of the two legs of a right triangle equals the square of the hypotenuse. A square number is the product of an integer multiplied by itself. Here we see that the length of the shortest leg is 3, and its square is 9. The length of the second leg is 4; its square is 16. The sum of 9 and 16 is 25. The length of the hypotenuse is 25, the square of 5.

81

Alexandrian scholars made breakthroughs in geometry, arithmetic, trigonometry, algebra, and applying mathematics to physical problems. Euclid, Archimedes, Eratosthenes, Dositheus, and Apollonius of Perga were among Alexandria's many mathematicians.

## Sieve of Eratosthenes

Eratosthenes and other Greeks were very interested in numbers. Many of their studies dealt with integers—whole numbers. They used fractions, but did not use decimal places. The Greeks distinguished between even and odd numbers. Even numbers, they noted, are whole numbers that can be divided by two. Odd numbers, they knew, are whole numbers that cannot be evenly divided into two groups. They found patterns that occur when even and odd numbers are added, subtracted, or multiplied— that even numbers multiplied by even numbers always resulted in even numbers. Even numbers multiplied by odd numbers also always yielded even numbers. They identified square numbers.

A square number is the product of another integer multiplied by itself, for example 4 x 4 = 16. Sixteen is the square number. Perfect numbers, triangular numbers, oblong numbers, and others were explored in ancient Greek studies of number theory.

Prime numbers were especially fascinating to the Greeks. A prime number is a whole number that can be evenly divided by no other whole number than one and itself. A prime number is a natural number—a positive integer. Fractions and negative numbers are not prime. The first prime numbers are 2, 3, 5, 7, 11, 13, 17, 19. (In that sequence of odd numbers, 9 is missing because it can be divided by 3; 15 is missing because it can be divided by 3 or 5.) There are no even prime numbers except for 2 because even numbers can always be divided by 2.

Patterns of prime numbers still elude and fascinate mathematicians. Many have tried to find patterns to predict when prime numbers occur. They have also looked for patterns of how frequently they occur. In one of Eratosthenes' books, he laid out a method that is now known as Eratosthenes's Sieve. This "sieve" is a systematic way to identify prime numbers. To find smaller prime numbers, the sieve can be laid out on a piece of paper. Many Web sites and computer programs carry the sieve to higher numbers.

| 1 | ② | 3 | 4 | 5 | 6 | 7 | 8 | 9 | 10 |
|---|---|---|---|---|---|---|---|---|---|
| 11 | 12 | 13 | 14 | 15 | 16 | 17 | 18 | 19 | 20 |
| 21 | 22 | 23 | 24 | 25 | 26 | 27 | 28 | 29 | 30 |
| 31 | 32 | 33 | 34 | 35 | 36 | 37 | 38 | 39 | 40 |
| 41 | 42 | 43 | 44 | 45 | 46 | 47 | 48 | 49 | 50 |
| 51 | 52 | 53 | 54 | 55 | 56 | 57 | 58 | 59 | 60 |
| 61 | 62 | 63 | 64 | 65 | 66 | 67 | 68 | 69 | 70 |
| 71 | 72 | 73 | 74 | 75 | 76 | 77 | 78 | 79 | 80 |
| 81 | 82 | 83 | 84 | 85 | 86 | 87 | 88 | 89 | 90 |
| 91 | 92 | 93 | 94 | 95 | 96 | 97 | 98 | 99 | 100 |

**Eratosthenes Sieve is a method to find prime numbers. In the first step of a sieve, every second integer after 2 is eliminated (Eliminated numbers shown here in red with diagonal hatch marks.)**

For a simple sieve, you can write the numbers from one to 100 on paper. It is easiest if you arrange them in columns, with 1 to 10 across the top row and subsequent sets of 10 lined up below. After your columns are arranged, you cross out every second integer excluding 2—in other words, all the even numbers except 2. Next start with 3, and cross out every third integer. Some of the integers, like 6 and 12 have already been crossed out. You still count them in your sequence. After completing the set for 3, start with the next uncrossed integer, which will be 5. Do not cross out 5, but this time count by 5's, eliminating 10, 15, et cetera. For 7's you will leave 7, but count by 7's, likewise 11, 13, and on through 97. When you have finished, the remaining numbers are all primes. You can see on your chart their irregular distribution.

## Doubling the Cube

The other mathematical work of Eratosthenes that we know about is his solution to a legendary Greek geometry problem. Several versions of this challenge are mentioned in Greek literature. According to one account, King Minos was upset that the tomb built for his son was too small. The tomb was one hundred feet on each side. Minos

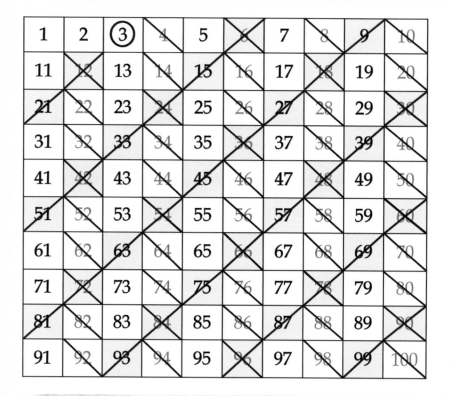

In the second step, every third number after 3 is eliminated. Those are shown shaded in blue. Subsequent steps start with the next uncrossed integer. Again, the first occurrence of the integer is not eliminated. Its multiples are crossed out as one proceeds.

wanted the volume of the tomb doubled.[5] A more famous version of the task is known as the Delian problem. The island of Delos was the birthplace of the god Apollo. Handsome temples there were dedicated to him. Of course, there was also an altar for offerings to the god. This altar was in the shape of a cube. Apollo reportedly demanded that his altar on Delos be doubled in size. To figure out the dimensions of the new altar, Apollo's priests went to the philosopher Plato at the Academy in Athens. Plato told the priests that the god had posed this difficult problem to reproach the Greeks for their lack of interest in geometry.[6]

At first glance, this looks like an easy problem to solve. A tiny bit of investigation, however, shows that it is really complex. If Apollo's altar was one meter on each side, then its volume would be one cubic meter. This is calculated by multiplying its height width and depth: 1 x 1 x 1. If the altar's dimensions were doubled to have two meters on each side, then the volume would be 2 x 2 x 2, or 8 cubic meters, obviously not double the original volume. Today we could approach this problem by finding the cube root of 2; we would probably use a calculator that included the cube root function to find our answer. However, in the pre-calculator Greek world, mathematicians like Eratosthenes looked to geometry.

The Delian problem had already been solved by a mathematician named Hippocrates (not the doctor of the same name) before Eratosthenes tackled it. Eratosthenes' fame here rests with finding a mechanical solution to the problem. He devised an instrument called a mesolabe that could calculate the answer. His device had a rectangular frame. Three triangles of the same height as the frame were set into it so they could slide and overlap each other. By moving the triangles, different proportions between the base, the height of the frame, and the diagonal created by the triangles yielded the correct answer.[7] One can imagine this device being similar to slide rules that can be used for many mathematical calculations.

To celebrate his discovery, Eratosthenes wrote a poem dedicated to the king, Ptolemy III. Eratosthenes explained that with his device it was not necessary to do the complicated mathematical calculations previously required to solve the Delian problem. In the poem, he described his invention and praised the king. Eratosthenes had his poem inscribed on a stone monument. The monument probably stood in a public place around the library or Museum. This type of monument and public announcement was not unusual. Greeks erected many public statues. For Eratosthenes, it was appropriate to dedicate his achievement to the king. The third Ptolemy had, after all, made him director of the library and supported Eratosthenes as a member of the royal court.

# 7

# TIME, POEMS, PLAYS, AND STARS

ANCIENT GREEKS ALREADY HAD MANY centuries of history when Eratosthenes was librarian at Alexandria. They had fought wars with Persia, and with each other. Cities had seen rule by tyrants like Gelon in Syracuse and kings like Cleomenes in Sparta. Athenians had heard memorable speeches in their public assemblies and had shaped democratic government. Occasional plagues and earthquakes had killed thousands. Poets, artists, and playwrights had been born, created masterpieces, and died. Sports heroes won fame for spectacular performances at the Olympics and other athletic competitions.

Greeks had a lot of history, but had no set

system for dating it. Today we can say that the American Declaration of Independence was signed in 1776, man first walked on the moon in 1969, and the Beijing Olympics were in 2008. Those dates, 1776, 1969, 2008, let us know the year when events occurred. The Greeks did not have a similar way to express years. Often their dates were connected to local events: the year that Themistocles became archon of Athens, or three years after the Battle of Marathon. A reference to a local ruler or date of a battle could be hard to interpret after much time had passed. Eratosthenes, with the same clear and organized approach he brought to other problems, established a chronology of Greek history. His text is known as Eratosthenes' *Chronological Tables*.

This chronology was set up as a detailed book of tables. It was not a narrative, or story of events. Eratosthenes drew from the histories and accounts on Alexandria's library shelves, including lists of Olympic victors.[1] The Olympic lists were very helpful, because these athletic contests took place every four years beginning in 776 B.C. These provided a framework that all Greeks knew. Eratosthenes then related other history to the Olympics. For example, with his chronology, he could say that he was born in the first year of the 126th Olympiad. That year, 276 B.C., was when the 126th games were held. The following years would be described as the second, third, and fourth years of the Olympiad. Next would be the first year of the 127th Olympiad, 272 B.C.[2]

In his chronology, Eratosthenes did not treat mythological happenings as history. His tables included political events, literary milestones, and cultural tidbits. Entertaining little facts of history and biography enlivened the lists. Although Eratosthenes' *Chronological Tables* no longer exists, we know that it was built upon by another Alexandrian scholar, Apollodorus of Athens. Apollodorus studied with Eratosthenes and continued some of his teacher's work. This chronology was the base that later scholars turned to for dates and many details of Greek history.

## Poet

Poems and plays formed a large part of the Alexandrian library collection. Many poets were there at the invitation of the Ptolemies. They wrote volumes upon volumes of poetry. Callimachus, Eratosthenes' countryman, wrote hundreds of poems: love poems, epics, hymns, funerary epigrams, and more.

Multitalented Eratosthenes also had a poetic side. Besides the epigram about doubling the cube, he wrote at least three other poems. History has preserved their names: *Hermes*, *Erigone*, and *Hesiod*. When writing about Homer, Eratosthenes had expressed the view that poetry was meant to delight, not to teach. That attitude may have set the tone for his compositions.

Eratosthenes' *Hermes* was about the Greek deity who was considered the messenger of the gods. A few lines of this poem survive. Several verses dealt with Hermes' childhood. At one point, the young god ascended into the heavens. There he saw heavenly spheres carrying the planets, sun, and moon around the earth. As Hermes looked down, he saw the earth's polar zones that "lie forever in the grip of ice." The area around the equator, Hermes saw, was "scorched with the rays of Maera the Dog Star." The temperate zones between these extremes were "mild and nurture the rich crops of Eleusian Demeter; in them dwell antipodean men."[3] His geography and astronomy shined in his artistic expression.

*Erigone* was based on a Greek legend about a father and daughter, Icarius and Erigone, and Erigone's dog, Maera. Icarius had been given the gift of cultivating grape vines by the god of wine, Dionysius. Tragedy befell Icarius and Erigone. In Eratosthenes' poem, he told how they became constellations in the night sky.[4] Maera became the star that is known today as Sirius, the Dog Star. The story of Icarius, Erigone, and Maera was part of an annual Greek festival, the Anthesteria.

Nothing is known about Eratosthenes' *Hesiod*. It seems likely that it was about the Greek poet of that name. Hesiod is credited with composing the *Theogony*, a poetic family tree of the gods, and *Works and Days*. *Works and Days* was a poetic calendar, with notes on agriculture, lucky days, and myths.

## Comedy

Not only were hundreds of plays on the shelves of Alexandria's library, troupes of actors performed them in the city's theaters. Eratosthenes seems to have had a particular fondness for classical Greek comedies, like those of Aristophanes. Aristophanes was a popular comic playwright. His witty plays satirized society and politics. A handful of his plays exist; they are still performed and still make audiences laugh and think.

Many scholars in Alexandria wrote about plays. They often listed and analyzed playwrights' vocabulary and choice of words. Eratosthenes took a different approach. His

*Ancient Comedy* had twelve essays on different theater topics. He discussed staging in one, and authorship of the comedies in another. He was very precise in his efforts to determine correct dates for plays, many of which had been written almost two centuries before his time. He apparently searched out historic references in them, details like a passing mention of a

Theater of Dionysus in Athens. Theater performances were social and festive events in ancient Greece, and competitions between performers and playwrights were features of festivals dedicated to the god Dionysus. In Alexandria, scholars including Eratosthenes studied and wrote about Greek plays.

statesman or a battle. With those nuggets, he could use Callimachus's *Tables* and his own chronology to try to fit the play into its correct year. Eratosthenes' *Ancient Comedy* was highly regarded and was mentioned in many Greek texts about theater.[5]

## Stars

When Eratosthenes, like other Greeks, looked up into the night sky, he saw a multitude of stars. We see most of these same stars more than twenty centuries later. The night sky has changed little during this time. The ancients, though, lived without artificial light. Even big cities like Alexandria and Athens fell dark after the sun had set. Nightly processions of stars, planets, and the moon were familiar to the Greeks. Through the year they knew that positions of stars, just like positions of the sun, signaled beginnings of seasons or times to harvest or plant.

Among the thousands of twinkling points of light in the heavens, certain stars and clusters of stars stood out to the Greeks. They began associating myths with groups of stars. By Eratosthenes' time the Greeks had populated the heavens with animals, heroes, and objects. Three serpents, two bears, two dogs, and an eagle, swan, and crow all found places aloft. A sea monster, dolphin, and three fish were identified with star groups. Other animals including a rabbit, crab, lion, and scorpion were there. Six heroes of Greek myths and two nymphs had homes in the heavens. A lock of hair, a ship, and a handful of other objects were also traced in the skies.[6] A collection of stars connected together to form a figure is called a constellation.

We do not how or when different constellations became part of the Greeks' lore. Homer, in the eighth century B.C., mentioned a few constellations in his poems. Other cultures including the Babylonians and Egyptians had constellations, but with their own stories and different star configurations. Greeks before Eratosthenes wrote about the heavens. Some writers described the locations of different star groups.

One of Eratosthenes' works was titled *Catasterisms*, which translates to "constellations." In his book, he compiled the myths associated with forty-eight Greek constellations. His text was apparently the first to give a thorough and organized account of these configurations and their myths.[7] The books of the Alexandrian library were undoubtedly valuable sources that helped Eratosthenes find many myths and stories of the heavens.

Eratosthenes' *Catasterisms* no longer exists. A

A map of the constellations from the astronomy studies of Claudius Ptolemy. This Ptolemy, no relation to the kings, lived in Alexandria in the first half of the second century A.D. This map shows the constellations whose myths were documented by Eratosthenes.

text of the same name, which includes forty-four stories, has survived. This work dates from the first or second century A.D. It is believed to be derived from Eratosthenes' original. Scholars refer to the author of this later work as Pseudo-Eratosthenes.[8] *Pseudo* means "pretend" or "counterfeit." Scholars still debate the connection between this text and Eratosthenes' original.

Reading the existing *Catasterisms* is like taking a tour of the heavens and meeting the figures of the Greeks. Concise stories tell about Orion the

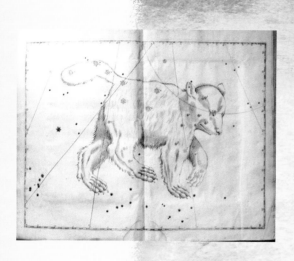

Map of the constellation Ursa Major, the big bear, from the 1600s. The stars that we know as the Big Dipper are in the bear's hip and tail.

hunter, Leo the lion, the dragon Draco, and others. The entries also tell who placed these creatures, heroes, and objects in the heavens and why they honored them. Hermes, the messenger god, put the rabbit in the sky to honor its speed. Poseidon, god of the sea, honored the dolphin because he helped him find his bride. Zeus, the most powerful of the gods, sent several figures, including the swan and the scorpion, to their heavenly posts.

Modern star maps identify the constellations of the ancient Greeks. Today, we can still go outside on a clear night and see the figures of Eratosthenes' *Catasterisms*.

# 8

# LEGACY

ERATOSTHENES DIED AROUND 200 B.C. or 195 B.C. It is sometimes said that he starved himself to death because he was going blind. Like so much about this remarkable man's life, we do not truly know the date or circumstances of his death.

The Library of Alexandria continued with a new director. Aristophanes of Byzantion succeeded Eratosthenes. Under his leadership and for the next few decades the library turned more to literature and language. Archimedes, Eratosthenes, and all of their generation of Alexandrian mathematicians and science-minded thinkers were gone. Over the decades, the library had high and low points, depending on the Ptolemies' support and interests. Soon, Rome was expanding and change was in the air.

In 48 B.C., after a series of battles, the Roman Emperor Julius Caesar was in Alexandria. The reigning Ptolemy of the time was young Cleopatra. Civil war was raging, and Caesar was surrounded in the palace complex. By some accounts, in order to keep back the armies and get himself and his troops to his ships, he burned the library. One Roman wrote, "Many places were set on fire, with the result that along with other buildings, the dockyards and the storehouses of grain and books, said to be great in number and of the finest, were burned."[1] Although books were lost in the fire, scholars believe that the library lasted longer, although not at its former greatness. The library likely continued to A.D. 270, when much of Alexandria was leveled in war.[2]

What happened then to the books and knowledge collected in Alexandria? Thousands of volumes were lost forever. Plays, poems, science, mathematics, geography, medical writings, and more burned or eventually crumbled with age. Some papyrus texts actually survived in the hot, dry sands of Egypt. In Oxyrhynchus, Egypt, thousands of papyri were discovered in the late 1800s. Many documented daily life—receipts for taxes, census counts, court decisions. A few lost literary works were unearthed there. Mathematical writings including a fragment with one of Euclid's propositions and a diagram were discovered in archaeological excavations.

Copies of some volumes from Alexandria migrated to other libraries and collections. A Greek library in Pergamum near the coast of Asia Minor was founded soon after Alexandria's library. The two institutions competed for scholars and prestige. In Pergamum, books began to be written in a different form. The scribes began copying their works onto parchment. Parchment is stretched and dried animal skin. Sheets of parchment were bound into books. Parchment was far more durable than papyrus. Through the centuries, much ancient Greek knowledge was preserved in parchment books. Some Greek books were kept in libraries in Rome. During the Middle Ages in Europe, Greek books were studied by Arab scholars. They were also kept in some monasteries.

With the European Renaissance, many Greek ideas were "rediscovered." In the mid-1400s, the invention of movable type printing press changed Europe. Instead of individual copies of texts being laboriously copied by hand, hundreds and even thousands of copies of a book could be produced. This sudden availability of written information must have been similar to the days in ancient Greece, when books first became available there. Literacy and hunger for knowledge spread quickly. Europeans rediscovered Greek literature, mathematics, philosophy, and science through books.

Although Eratosthenes' own writings did not make it to this point in history, his ideas did, and they were carried on into the modern world. They were brought forward in the texts and in the achievements of Strabo, Cleomedes, Apollodorus, and Pseudo-Eratosthenes, as well as countless other geographers, mathematicians, astronomers, poets, historians, theater critics, and even philosophers who he had influenced. Eratosthenes' approach to describing the world was a foundation built upon by later geographers. His chronology gave generations a better picture of antiquity. Eratosthenes' application of mathematics to geography opened the door to better understanding of our planet. His calculation of the earth's circumference was amazingly accurate. With it, he showed that the earth, like other objects, had limits and could be measured. As director of the Library of Alexandria, he nurtured the culture of learning there.

Christopher Columbus disagreed with Eratosthenes' measurement. Yet Columbus's expeditions and the Age of Exploration were built upon a global view that had roots back to Eratosthenes. Today, when we look at our understanding of the world and its geography, we still have connections to this remarkable multitalented ancient Greek.

# ACTIVITIES

## Sundials and Shadows

Eratosthenes measured the circumference of the earth using mathematics and one basic device—a sundial. You can make a simple sundial. With it, you can observe interconnections between the sun and the earth as the earth rotates on its axis and revolves around the sun.

**Materials:**

- ❖ a piece of flat cardboard, about one foot long and wide
- ❖ a plastic drinking straw, cut to about 4 inches long
- ❖ tape
- ❖ a pen, pencil, or marker

**Procedure:**

Tape the drinking straw to the cardboard so that it stands vertically from the cardboard. The straw is the gnomon of your sundial.

On a clear day, preferably in the morning, set your sundial outside in the sunlight. Set it in a location where it will be in the sun for most of the day. You want to choose a place where you can set it up again on later days in the same position. It needs to be in the same position each day you observe—with the same edge of the cardboard pointing north. To assure that it is in the same position, you might line up one edge of it with the edge of a driveway or bricks on a patio and make a note to yourself on the cardboard.

When you first set your sundial outside, observe the length of the shadow cast by your gnomon. Mark the end of the shadow. With that mark, note the date and time. If your sundial is in a place where it will not be disturbed, anchor it with a couple of stones or other weights and leave it there for several hours. When you return, mark the length of the later shadow. If it is convenient, try to observe your sundial at around noon when the shadow will be at its shortest. Try to mark three or four observations on your first day.

After the first day, put your sundial safely away and wait a couple of weeks. Set it up again in exactly the same position. Again record the length of the shadow at three or four different times of day.

What does the gnomon's shadow reveal on a single day? It shows the earth's counterclockwise rotation that appears as the sun's movement through the sky. In the morning the sun is in the eastern sky and casts a shadow to the west. At around noon the sun is in its highest position and casts its shortest shadow. In the afternoon and evening, the sun is seen in the western sky while the shadow falls to the east.

What is revealed by observations taken on a series of dates? From the relative lengths of the gnomon's shadows, you will see if the sun is moving higher in the sky and casting shorter shadows or lower in the sky and casting longer ones. If the shadows are getting shorter, you are moving toward summer.

There are two times each year when you could make your observations and find shadows of the same length on two separate days a couple of weeks apart. If you make your observations an equal number of days before and after the solstice, the shadows will be the same length. On the solstices (around June 21 and December 21) the sun reaches its extreme positions and then begins its retreat to its other extreme.

❖   Hint: You will find the greatest difference in the shadows if you observe around the equinoxes—March 21 and October 21.

## Make a Sieve

In Chapter 6, you saw the Sieve of Eratosthenes for numbers one to 100. You can make a sieve that goes even higher. With it you will find even more prime numbers.

Try laying out a sieve with numbers from one to 300. Arrange them in columns, with 1 to 10 across the top row and subsequent sets of 10 lined up below. After your columns are arranged, cross out every second integer excluding 2. You can eliminate entire columns of even numbers. For the next step, cross out every third integer except number 3. Some of the integers, like 6 and 12 have already been crossed out. You still count them in your sequence. After completing the set for 3, start with the next uncrossed integer which will be 5. Do not cross out 5, but this time count by 5s, eliminating 10, 15 et cetera. For 7s you will leave 7, but count by 7s, likewise 11, 13, and on to complete your sieve. When you have finished, the remaining numbers are all primes.

There are several outstanding online sieves that can be used to search for higher prime numbers.

## Stars and Stories

A familiar sight in the Northern Hemisphere night sky is the Big Dipper. Connecting the dots of its seven bright stars, one finds the shape of a ladle or long-handled pot. In some countries it is considered a plow or a wagon. Some African traditions saw it as a drinking gourd, a water dipper. During the American Civil War, slaves who were trying to escape southern states would "follow the drinking gourd," because this group of stars pointed to the north and the hope of freedom.

The Big Dipper is an asterism, a grouping of stars that is not an official constellation. Yet, it has a rich history of legends, myths, and meaning. The Big Dipper's stars are in the constellation Ursa Major, the "Big Bear" of the ancient Greeks.

Over the centuries, many cultures had myths and stories tied to the stars. The Greeks' myths, though, provided the framework used to identify different areas in the heavens. In 1930, the International Astronomical Union adopted an official list of eighty-eight constellations, whose borders include every point in the sky. The Greeks' constellations live on in this official list.

To begin learning about constellations, start

**111**

A nighttime photo of Ursa Major ("The Big Dipper").

by observing the night sky. On a clear night, find a quiet place with a good view of the night sky. Visibility is best on nights with no moon. Look at the stars and see which groups stand out to your eyes. You may see the Big Dipper or the three bright stars in a row that are Orion's Belt. Orion was a Greek hunter put in the heavens by Zeus. If you can see the Big Dipper, you can use the image on page 100 to find the Greeks' Ursa Major. The Big Dipper's stars form the bear's hip and tail. Fainter stars mark the points of its head and legs.

There are some bright stars in the Greeks' constellations, but their full patterns are difficult to recognize without a map. Maps of the constellations are available online and in bookstores.

# CHRONOLOGY

**c. 630 B.C.**—Cyrene is founded by Greeks from Thera.

**c. 530 B.C.**—Greek philosopher Pythagoras considers the earth a globe.

**384–322 B.C.**—Among Aristotle's many studies are discussions of the earth's spherical shape and size.

**332 B.C.**—Alexandria, Egypt, is founded by Alexander the Great.

**323 B.C.**—Alexander the Great dies.

**305 B.C.**—Ptolemy I becomes king of Egypt, founding the Greek dynasty that would rule there for almost three centuries. Formerly a trusted general under Alexander the Great, Ptolemy I was also an historian who wrote histories of Alexander's military campaigns. The Library and Museum of Alexandria are likely founded during his reign.

**282 B.C.**—Ptolemy II succeeds his father as king of Egypt. He continues to build the library collection and attracts scholars to Alexandria. He completes the Pharos lighthouse.

**c. 276 B.C.**—Eratosthenes is born in Cyrene.

**c. 258 B.C.**—Eratosthenes goes to Athens to study.

**246 B.C.**—Ptolemy III becomes king of Egypt and marries a princess from Cyrene.

**c. 245 B.C.**—Eratosthenes moves to Alexandria at the invitation of Ptolemy III and becomes chief librarian at Library of Alexandria. He likely remains chief librarian for most of the rest of his life. He does his studies of geography, Earth's circumference, mathematics, chronology, constellations, theater, and more at Alexandria.

**c. 195 B.C.**—Eratosthenes dies.

**c. 63 B.C.–A.D. 24**—Greek geographer Strabo's lifetime. Strabo's *Geography* includes much information about Eratosthenes' works.

**50 B.C.–A.D. 200**—Sometime during this period, Cleomenes writes about the heavens, including a description of Eratosthenes' method of measuring the earth's circumference.

**48 B.C.**—Fire in Alexandria destroys warehouses including some of library collection.

**A.D. 270**—Probable end of Alexandria's library.

## CHAPTER NOTES

### Chapter 1. "Pentathlos"

1. Samuel Eliot Morison, *Admiral of the Ocean Sea* (Boston: Little Brown and Company, 1942), vol. 1, pp. 120–121.

2. Ibid., pp. 122–123.

3. O. A. W. Dilke, *Greek and Roman Maps* (Ithaca, N.Y.: Cornell University Press, 1985), pp. 32–33.

4. *Dictionary of Scientific Biography*, s.v. "Eratosthenes" (by D. R. Dicks).

### Chapter 2. Boy From Cyrene

1. Catherine B. Avery, ed., *The New Century Classical Handbook* (New York: Appleton-Century-Crofts, 1962), pp. 351–352.

2. Paul Cartledge, ed., *The Cambridge Illustrated History of Ancient Greece* (New York: Cambridge University Press, 1998), pp. 328–329.

3. P. M. Fraser, *Ptolemaic Alexandria* (Oxford: Clarendon Press, 1972), p. 151.

4. Ken Parejko, "Pliny the Elder's Silphium: First Recorded Species Extinction," *Conservation Biology*, vol. 17, no. 3, June 2003, pp. 925–926.

5. James Gow, *A Short History of Greek Mathematics* (New York: Chelsea Publishing, 1884, revised reprint 1968), p. 174.

6. *Dictionary of Scientific Biography*, s.v. "Eratosthenes" (by D. R. Dicks).

### Chapter 3. Alexandria

1. Theodore Vrettos, *Alexandria: City of the Mind* (New York: The Free Press, 2001), pp. 31–32.

2. Catherine B. Avery, ed., *The New Century Classical Handbook* (New York: Appleton-Century-Crofts, 1962), p. 79.

3. Lionel Casson, *Libraries in the Ancient World* (New Haven, Conn.: Yale University Press, 2001), p. 32.

4. P. M. Fraser, *Ptolemaic Alexandria* (Oxford: Clarendon Press, 1972), p. 15.

5. David Whitehouse, "Library of Alexandria Discovered," *BBC News*, May 12, 2004, <http://news.bbc.co.uk/1/hi/sci/tech/3707641.stm> (July 5, 2008).

6. Avery, p. 456.

7. Casson, pp. 35–36.

8. Ibid., p. 36.

9. Ibid., p. 18.

10. Ibid., p. 19.

11. John Boardman, Jasper Griffen, and Oswyn Murray, eds., *The Oxford History of the Greek World* (New York: Oxford University Press, 1986), p. 350.

12. Fraser, p. 452.

13. Ibid., p. 325.

14. Casson, p. 38.

## Chapter 4. Measuring the Earth

1. Aristotle, *On the Heavens I & II*, trans. and ed. Stuart Leggatt (Warminster, England: Aris & Phillips, 1995), pp. 167–169.

2. Ibid.

3. Alan Bowen and Robert Todd, eds., *Cleomedes' Lectures on Astronomy* (Berkeley: University of California Press, 2004), p. 3.

4. Strabo, *The Geography of Strabo*, trans. Horace Leonard Jones, The Loeb Classical Library, vol. 1 (New York: G. P. Putnam's Sons, 1917), p. 233.

5. Bowen and Todd, pp. 81–82.

6. Ibid., p. 82.

7. Strabo, vol. 8, p. 129.

8. Bowen and Todd, p. 82.

9. Ibid., pp. 83–84.

10. P. M. Fraser, *Ptolemaic Alexandria* (Oxford: Clarendon Press, 1972), p. 415.

11. Geoffrey J. Martin, *All Possible Worlds: A History of Geographical Ideas*, 4th ed. (New York: Oxford University Press, 2005), p. 32.

12. Fraser, pp. 413–414.

13. *Dictionary of Scientific Biography*, s.v. "Eratosthenes" (by D. R. Dicks).

## Chapter 5. Geography

1. *Dictionary of Scientific Biography*, s.v. "Eratosthenes" (by D. R. Dicks).

2. O. A. W. Dilke, *Greek and Roman Maps* (Ithaca, N.Y.: Cornell University Press, 1985), p. 12.

3. Geoffrey J. Martin, *All Possible Worlds: A History of Geographical Ideas*, 4th ed. (New York: Oxford University Press, 2005), pp. 28–29.

4. Strabo, *The Geography of Strabo*, trans. Horace Leonard Jones, The Loeb Classical Library, vol. 1 (New York: G. P. Putnam's Sons, 1917), p. 259.

5. Ibid., vol. 1, xxv.

6. P. M. Fraser, *Ptolemaic Alexandria* (Oxford: Clarendon Press, 1972), p. 526.

7. Strabo, vol. 1, p. 51.

8. Ibid., vol. 1, p. 55.

9. Ibid., vol. 1, p. 67.

10. Ibid., vol. 1, p. 59.

11. Fraser, p. 529.

12. Strabo, vol. 1, p. 313.

13. Fraser, p. 533.

14. Strabo, vol. 1, p. 249.

15. Fraser, p. 624.

## Chapter 6. Mathematician

1. E. J. Dijksterhuis, *Archimedes* (Princeton, N.J.: Princeton University Press, 1938), p. 314.

2. Thomas L. Heath, *A History of Greek Mathematics* (Oxford: Clarendon Press, 1921), p. 105.

3. P. M. Fraser, *Ptolemaic Alexandria* (Oxford: Clarendon Press, 1972), p. 410.

4. Howard Eves, *An Introduction to the History of Mathematics*, 3rd ed. (New York: Holt, Rinehart and Winston, 1953), p. 50.

5. Fraser, p. 411.

6. Ibid., p. 410.

7. Thomas L. Heath, *A Manual of Greek Mathematics* (New York: Dover Publications, 1931), pp. 162–164.

## Chapter 7. Time, Poems, Plays, and Stars

1. P. M. Fraser, *Ptolemaic Alexandria* (Oxford: Clarendon Press, 1972), p. 457.

2. E. J. Bickerman, *Chronology of the Ancient World* (Ithaca, N.Y.: Cornell University Press, 1968), p. 147.

3. Fraser, p. 624.

4. Ibid., p. 641.

5. Ibid., p. 457.

6. Theony Condos, *Star Myths of the Greeks and Romans: A Sourcebook* (Grand Rapids, Mich.: Phanes Press, 1997), p. 24.

7. Ibid., p. 20.

8. Ibid., p. 19.

## Chapter 8. Legacy

1. Lionel Casson, *Libraries in the Ancient World* (New Haven, Conn.: Yale University Press, 2001), p. 46.

2. Ibid., p. 47.

# GLOSSARY

**agora**—An ancient Greek marketplace.

**antipodean**—Of opposite sides of the earth.

**base line**—An imaginary line running east and west crossing a meridian at a specific point.

**buoyancy**—The power to keep something afloat.

**chronology**—The science of locating events in time and arranging events in order of their occurrence.

**circumference**—The distance around a circle.

**circumscribe**—To encompass or encircle.

**constellation**—A group of stars that are connected together to form a picture.

**eclipse**—The partial or total obscuring of one celestial body by another. In a lunar eclipse, the earth passes directly between the sun and moon, casting its shadow on the moon.

**epigram**—A short poem.

**geography**—A descriptive science dealing with the earth, its division into continents and countries, and the climate, plants, animals, natural resources, inhabitants, and industries of the various divisions.

**gnomon**—The column or pin on a sundial.

**grammarian**—An expert in grammar.

**hypotenuse**—The longest side of a right triangle.

**integer**—Any positive or negative whole number or zero.

**latitude**—A measurement of angular distance on the earth north or south of the equator.

**longitude**—A measurement expressed in degrees or time of angular distance on the earth east or west of a set meridian. Today, longitude is measured from the prime meridian that runs through Greenwich, England.

**mean**—The midpoint between the extreme numbers in a set; an average.

**meridian line**—A great circle passing through the north and south poles and any point on the earth's surface.

**mesolabe**—An instrument used by the ancients to find the mean proportionals between two given lines.

**myriad**—To the ancient Greeks, ten thousand.

**papyrus**—A Mediterranean plant that can be made into a form of paper.

**prime number**—Any whole number greater than one that has only two factors, one and itself.

**proportion**—In mathematics, a statement of equality between two ratios.

**sanctuary**—A place set aside for worship of a deity or deities.

**scaphe**—A bowl sundial with a vertical gnomon inside of it, used for timekeeping. The gnomon's shadow could be followed on curved lines inside the bowl.

**scriptorium**—A room for copying manuscripts.

**silphium**—An extinct plant that grew in the region around Cyrene, Libya.

**solstice**—From the Latin words for sun (sol) and stand (sistere) meaning when the sun stands still. The solstice is the moment when the sun in its apparent annual movement reaches its maximum distance north or south. The solstices occur around June 21 and December 21. In the Northern Hemisphere the day of the June solstice has the longest amount of sunlight and the sun reaches its highest point in the sky.

**stade**—A distance measurement in ancient Greece.

**talent**—A unit of weight, often of silver, used as money in ancient Greece.

**tome**—A volume or work of several volumes, often a large or scholarly work.

**tropical circle**—Either of two parallels on the earth representing the points farthest north and south of the equator at which the sun can shine directly overhead.

**tyrant**—An absolute ruler.

# FURTHER READING

Casson, Lionel. *Libraries in the Ancient World*. New Haven, Conn.: Yale University Press, 2001.

Condos, Theony. *Star Myths of the Greek and Romans: A Sourcebook*. Grand Rapids, Mich.: Phanes Press, 1997. This includes translation of Pseudo-Eratosthenes' *Catasterisms*.

Nicastro, Nicholas. *Circumference: Eratosthenes and the Ancient Quest to Measure the Globe*. New York: St. Martin's Press, 2008.

Trumble, Kelly. *The Library of Alexandria*. New York: Clarion Books, 2003.

# INTERNET ADDRESSES

**Eratosthenes biography, University of St. Andrews (Scotland)**
http://www-history.mcs.st-andrews.ac.uk/history/
    Biographies/Eratosthenes.html

**Eratosthenes of Cyrene, Univeristy of Utah**
http://www.math.utah.edu/~pa/Eratosthenes.html

**The Eratoshtenes Project, Sonoma State University**
http://phys-astro.sonoma.edu/observatory/
    eratosthenes/

# INDEX